Oct. 31, 2010

To Doris, good friend & neighbour, with best wishes! Mary A Mulhern

Sleeping with Satan
Salem Witch-hunt, 1692

Mary Ann Mulhern

Black Moss
Press
2010

Library and Archives Canada Cataloguing in Publication

Mulhern, Mary Ann
    Sleeping with Satan / Mary Ann Mulhern.

Poems.
ISBN 978-0-88753-469-0

    I. Title.

PS8576.U415S54 2010   C811'.6   C2010-902232-7

Cover artwork: Naomi Hughes, used with permission
Design: Karen Veryle Monck

Published by Black Moss Press at 2450 Byng Road, Windsor, Ontario, N8W
3E8. Canada. Black Moss books are distributed in Canada and the U.S. by
LitDistCo. All orders should be directed there.

Black Moss would like to acknowledge the generous financial support from
both the Canada Council for the Arts and the Ontario Arts Council.

ONTARIO ARTS COUNCIL
CONSEIL DES ARTS DE L'ONTARIO

Le Conseil des Arts | The Canada Council
du Canada | for the Arts

PRINTED IN CANADA

*For all the women who died on Gallow's Hill
and for women who are being unfairly persecuted today.*

ACKNOWLEDGEMENTS

"Choking on a Curse" and "Miscarriage" will be published in the 2011 spring edition of the *Windsor Review*.

Marty Gervais mentored me with the Salem poems and encouraged me to continue to research and write about these tragic events in Salem, Massachusetts, in 1692.

Janine Morris and Danielle Romanello edited these poems with skill and dedication. Their work has been detailed and informed, and has greatly contributed to the creative focus, design and structure of this book.

John B. Lee gave me creative insights and direction for the poem "Stone-Cold Cradle".

The Writers Salon helped me shape several of these poems.

Penny-Anne Beaudoin was a constant source of encouragement and advice. She was always ready to answer questions, and to offer suggestions.

Anne-Marie Charron, from the beginning sent websites with extremely helpful information and historical background.

Amber Pinsonneault read this manuscript and made several valuable suggestions which are reflected in these poems.

Dr. Pam Milne's classes on "Women and Religion" were the inspiration for these poems. Her knowledge of history gave me insights into the hysteria and hatred that caused the deaths of so many innocent women, which sadly continues into the present-day violence against women.

My family and friends have offered a great deal of support, especially by the continuing interest they have shown in this work.

TABLE OF CONTENTS

Prologue	9
The Witch House	11
Gallow's Hill	12
Bewitchment	13
Secrets of a Sorceress	14
An Orphan of Fortune	15
Abigail's Adultery	16
Dressed in the Devil's Silk	17
A Young Girl's Craze	18
Tangled in a Purple Cord	19
Virgins of Salem	20
Blight	21
Spectral Witness	22
Amulet	23
Secrets of Voodoo	24
French Lace	25
Dark Hand	26
Sunday Service of Martha Corey	27
With My Sharpest Knife	28
Communion of Magic	29
Believer	30
Magic Charm	31
Testimony of Abigail Williams	32
Sounds of Sorcery	33
Exposed	34
Inside Out	35

Rebecca's Silence   36
A Servant Speaks   37
Petition of Mary Easty   38
Refusal to Confess   39
Sleeping with Satan   40
Outside   41
In the Dust   42
Miscarriage   43
Court-Cold Cradle   44
Four-Year-Old Witch   45
Prison Death   46
Hunger and Thirst   47
Skeleton   48
From the Scaffold   49
Early Frost   50
Choking on a Curse   51
When my Mother Dies   53
Last Breath of Leaves   54
Chains   55
Doubt   56
A Witch with Wings   57
Abigail Williams in Boston   58
Too late   59
Absolution   60
Playing Field   62
Glossary   63

I will not plead

If I deny, I am condemned already,

In courts where ghosts appear as witnesses,

And swear men's lives away. If I confess,

Then I confess a lie, to buy a life

Which is not life, but only death in life.

William Wadsworth Longfellow

Prologue

From June through October 1692, in Salem, Massachusetts, one-hundred and fifty people were charged and nineteen people were convicted of witchcraft and hanged on Gallow's Hill for refusing to plead guilty. Beginning in Salem, the witch-hunt eventually spread to twenty-four neighboring towns by its end in October.

The accusations of witchcraft began when several teenage girls accused three women of bewitching them. The girls making the accusations of witchcraft included Abigail Williams, Ann Putnam, Mercy Lewis, Mary Walcott, Mary Warren, Elizabeth Booth, Susannah Sheldon, and Tituba. Their evidence rested on spectral testimonies, or the accuser's claims that they witnessed the spirit of the accused engaging in a malicious or harmful act. These acts could include causing blight, a plague, or flood, as well as physically attacking the accuser. It was believed that an individual's specter, or spirit, could only be seen because the individual had consented with the devil.

In April of 1692, a special court was created by Massachusetts governor William Phips in order to manage the increasing accusations, which at this point was nearing fifty. Only individuals who refused to confess were executed; the ones who chose to confess were spared to assist in the accusations of others.

Courtroom scenes were a spectacle, with young girls chanting and swooning before judges, claiming that the spirit of the accused was attacking them in that moment. These demonstrations were considered proof of witchcraft and the accused was condemned to be hanged on these grounds.

An accused witch was not allowed legal counsel, nor could she speak in her own defense. Anyone who did speak to the defense of the accused also risked being accused of witchcraft. Confessions resulted in the names of the accused being nailed across the door of the Puritan church, thus shaming their families and resulting in the seizure of their property.

The witchcraft hysteria ended abruptly when Lady Mary Phips was accused of witchcraft. The governor promptly appealed to the higher courts in Boston who deemed spectral witness claims no longer admissible which led to the end of the witch trials.

Years later, the United States government sent financial compensation to families of those who had been wrongly executed.

The poems in this collection draw from historical fact but some are fictionalized in order to bridge the gap between meaning and history.

THE WITCH HOUSE

cloaked in black
a young tour guide
proclaims my story
to anyone who'll pay
I was built
in the center of Salem
in November, 1660
sturdy enough to withstand
every storm but one
my rooms opened
into a court of witches
nineteen of them
refused to confess
before the honourable
Jonathan Corwin
the judge who ordered each
weighted down with chains
led through weathered doors
to a hawthorn branch
jeers of Gallow's Hill
nineteen names echo still
in the gray moldings
of high ceilings

not guilty
not guilty
not guilty

Gallow's Hill

my body spins
in an August wind
lips swollen blue
shamed remnant of Salem
left to the mercy of the moon
sudden swoop of bats
cruel theft of crows

long after midnight
my husband cuts me down
carries me to a grave
concealed between distant trees
unmarked
unmapped
a burial without scripture
or prayer or hymn
only one mourner to weep
a witch is forbidden
to rest in holy ground
her bones a desecration
evil roots of magic
creeping over grass
bearing blooms
translucent white
pure as any rose
in paradise

BEWITCHMENT

Betty Parris, child of the minister
only six summers since birth
begins to scream in the house
the church, the meeting hall
every night she cowers
in corners shadowed by stars
cheeks and eyes fevered red
tongue blistered with fear

she cannot speak
the doctor suspects
she is bewitched
Satan in the streets
his witches casting spells
changing children into creatures
who must be caged
as young as six

SECRETS OF A SORCERESS

I am Tituba
dark-skinned, exotic
stolen
from an island
a preacher's concubine
in cushions of day
pillows of night

Puritan girls
close sacred books
embrace the spell
of my shameless dance
wings of magic
shimmer in their eyes
they ponder my words
secrets the Bible fears
how a woman can hold
the moon in her hands
read the Devil's script

An Orphan of Fortune

I am an orphan
servant in a Puritan house
a cramped attic room
shared with bats
crusts of bread
rinds of cheese
one pair of shoes
two dresses drab as dust
patched with shame

a dangerous slave
foretells my future
secrets she borrows
from Satan
the man who'll marry me
daughters and sons
from our marriage bed
enough to fill
empty spaces left by
my mother, my father
buried in a battle
sharpened arrows aimed
at weary hearts of settlers
whose only claim
is a barren grave

ABIGAIL'S ADULTERY

late at night
John Proctor stares
from his window
watches me on the swing
the way I glide, back and forth
breasts unbound, legs apart
long hair brushed with the moon

he grasps my hand
leads me to soft, clean straw
nested in his barn
our mating is brutal
wild as beasts in the hills

I've felt his eyes trace my body
in the meeting hall, the church
a sixteen-year old servant
who knows how to bargain
for all the polished rooms
of another woman's house

I've made him wait
all these months

DRESSED IN THE DEVIL'S SILK

just before midnight
Puritan men
appear at my tavern tables
thirsty for the taste
of forbidden ale
their wives sleep
with cotton bonnets
on their dreamless heads
I move table to table
scarlet feathers
blaze around my face
my rounded breasts

I know Puritan hearts
how they cover
all that sin
how they turn me
into a witch
dressed in the Devil's silk
until I am hung
high enough
for all of them
to breathe

A Young Girl's Craze

the tongue of a slave
preaches voodoo
spells stolen
from the Devil's hand
her words burrow deep
I thirst
for one hour
in a courtroom
where I dance
a young girl's craze
where I speak
names of witches
women I accuse
before a judge
persuasion
of my virgin body
hair flying wild
smooth, shiny strands
lies that curl
into a rope

Tangled in a Purple Cord

I birth
a village child
small , perfect body
tangled in a purple cord

his absence of breath
fills the room
the house
I bury the placenta
burn the caul

rumours fly
from windows and doors
this midwife
draws death
from wombs
cold and silent
and still

Virgins of Salem

the moon
swirls golden skirts
in the Salem Sea
seven of us dance
join in forbidden rites
Tituba stands naked
a proud goddess
hands open to receive
blessings of the night
a topaz amulet
flawless on her flesh
she commands us
to cast off
petticoats and skirts
tight bindings
of the Bible's loom
to let light play
on virgin breasts
an invitation to Satan

the only angel

Blight

overnight
every apple turns brown
splits open
spills useless seeds
on the ground
my footprints
are there
fresh from yesterday
when I walked
beneath a hundred trees
reached for ripened fruit
my hand a curse

I've become a witch
spoiled apple
saved for the gibbet
all that flesh
left to swell
wrinkled and bruised

easy to peel

SPECTRAL WITNESS

just beyond my window
over fields
half-lit by the moon
I feel her presence
Sarah Good
thin hair licked by cats
she's there among cattle
huddled close in the rain
she gently feeds
each pregnant cow
from pockets
stuffed with poisoned grain

milk mingles with blood
summer pasture seeds
a winter grave
white-faced calves curl
into sunken wombs
eyes forever closed
to openings of birth

Amulet

I pray
for enough magic
to disappear
ride a river of rage
dive beneath the sea
wash up
on the edge of heaven
or the east side
of hell
I pray for a topaz amulet
radiant as the moon's
midnight smile

Secrets of Voodoo

Abigail Williams sews a doll
long flowered skirt
lace petticoats
every stitch measured
with hate for me
wife of the man
who scorns her

beneath the starched bodice
she hides a needle
mean as any blade
embedded in the chest
where my heart beats blood
red drops of suspicion
evidence for the magistrate
who charges me
a witch who keeps
secrets of voodoo
hidden in a faceless doll
that begins to breathe
to witness against me

FRENCH LACE

the Salem dyer
fingers lace
too fine for a Puritan
too loose for purity
he watches it turn
from white
to scarlet, indigo and black
colours I choose
to cover my breasts
brush against nipples
enough for a witch
to draw any man
into her red, red circle

DARK HAND

in the church
a shadow passes
moves along the wall
I know
my accuser is here
among those who kneel
who worship their God
tomorrow I'll be called
to the meeting room
he'll be there
the one who covets
harvests of my land
whose wife
measures my house
every window and door
marked by her eye
all those empty rooms

echoes of a witch

SUNDAY SERVICE OF MARTHA COREY

young girls
enter the church
bow their heads
hide sins of malice
in a house of God

I begin to read
from the holy text
Abigail Williams and Ann Putman
smile
they've heard me deny
witches, spectral witness
 hangings on Gallow's Hill

I feel their eyes
flash over my face
my home-spun dress
dry breasts beneath
in silence the girls mock me
they have found a verse
they can chant in a dirge
knowing my fate
arises from scripture

you must not suffer a witch
to live

With My Sharpest Knife

I hear talk
of a witch
I become afraid
of cats and spiders and birds
all those eyes
watching me
knowing I have hidden
a bruised blemish
on my thigh
if I cut it out
with my sharpest knife
they will see blood
how my wound festers
some will say
there are maggots
breeding in my flesh
spreading into cradles
and marriage beds
sentinels of death
spawn of Satan's whore

COMMUNION OF MAGIC

my daughter, Abigail,
child of a tilted womb
refuses to visit
my filthy cell
to wash my clothes
bring milk, pudding and cheese

hunger, sickness and cold
silence bold words of innocence
they hand me a confession
I, Deliverance Hobbs
served red wine
and red bread
at gatherings of witches
a communion of magic
where we knelt
before Satan
his many angels

I scratch my name
across the page
proof of danger
hags in untrimmed bonnets
hand-stitched dresses
neighbours who share
food and drink
with the Devil
in dustless rooms
on every street

Believer

I embrace magic
I know how to tie
perfect knots of hate
bless them with a witch's kiss
hide them between
shoots of summer corn
watch three black candles
flame in the eye of a storm

I'll be found out
condemned in their court
I've saved one candle
for the judge
bitter tallow of grief
held the death card
in the pulse of my palm
every bone of the skull
grinning

Magic Charm

in the courtroom
a witness says
I've sewn
a magic charm
beneath the skin
of my left arm
the Devil's gift
the judge clutches
a leather pouch
worn around his neck
herbs preserved with wax
to ward off spells
cast from the shine
of hair and eyes and lips
I smell his potion
crushed hawthorn leaves
and fruit
rich-red and green
taken from the tree
that offers branches
high and wide and strong
enough for the swing
of a wealthy witch
her prison gown
blown into a blossom
tossed over a grave

Testimony Of Abigail Williams

when night takes hold
of earth
she comes to me
Martha Corey, the Gospel Woman
who leads Sunday prayer
in a Puritan church
scrubbed clean of sex and greed
she dips my finger
in blood
commands me to sign
the Devil's book
to partake
of his sacrament
my throat refuses breath
my body falls
into a silent space
the witch drags me
down spirals of smoke
towards tunnels of fire

Sounds of Sorcery

both of my taverns
thrive
in a parched Puritan town
my brother-in-law
broods
sips long, slow drafts
bitter on his tongue

in a Salem court
he testifies to sounds of sorcery
laughter in the night
he's seen the Devil's lips
hot upon my breasts
heard me whisper promises
into Satan's ear

Exposed

women tear open
my red Parisian dress
examination of a witch
the judge leans forward
his whole body sweats desire
girls clothed in white
whirl around the room
chanting my name
Bridget Byshop
Bridget Byshop
Bridget Byshop

I stand at a precipice
deny, deny, deny
charges of Satan's spit
smeared on cradles
babies scarred with pox
jurors scribble

guilty guilty guilty

Inside Out

I wear hats
with golden plumes
my bodice scarlet
roses threaded
round and high
sultry underskirts
edged with lace

in a Salem court
my clothes turn me
inside out
a witch hidden
in silky seams
sewn by
the Devil's hand

on Gallow's Hill
my eyes feed
a midnight owl
my dress lines
nests of crows
torn lace
trailing down

Rebecca's Silence

I have seen seventy winters
and summers both
now my ears silence
all the sounds
of earth

the judge asks me
a question
I cannot hear
my bewildered nod
signals guilt

the woodland owl
swallows wounded prey
a noisy crow taunts
the bleak scaffold
of dawn

A Servant Speaks

in the Proctor's house
I am an apron
starched stiff and plain
every meal spooned
from small bowls
chipped with charity

in the courtroom
I reveal myself, Mary Warren,
an angel of salvation
I have seen Satan
walking hand in hand
with Elizabeth Proctor
witnessed their plot
of plague and flood
and fire
on my words
my mistress stands condemned
sentenced to the scaffold
her eyes already closed
her body turned to stone

I sign a copy of my words
scripted large and round
letters slant into lies
settle in my soul
take root

Petition of Mary Easty

my hand reaches for a pen
paper white as death
waiting for my words
testament of innocence
my accusers shape lies
into steps of a courtroom dance
spells of the two-faced moon
young girls chant names
of condemned witches
hanged from a Salem rope
knots threaded with thorns

I plead for release
from the shame of this cell
stain of my prison dress
the judge folds my plea
into a lonely scaffold
where I can barely stand
blots of ink blind the sun
every star in a Godless sky

Refusal To Confess

rope tightens around my neck
presses against the pulse
of my throat
loops around a high branch
a serpent sent to strangle me
there is poison in the crowd
fangs and tongues
that hiss at a witch
who refuses to confess
the evil one whose eye
shone on this year's crops
shrivelled apples and pears
wilted ears of corn
wasted kernels
scattered on the ground

my hand could never hold the pen
all those letters of my name
nailed to the door of a church
scrawled across the forehead of my child
screamed by birds circling
a ghost covered with snow
illusion of a murdered bride

Sleeping with Satan

these Puritans study scripture
all those passages about
my tricks and lies and snares
men who think
I'd sin with white-haired hags
when there are young girls
who love to dance
to test their charms
loose tresses of hair
breasts not yet swollen with milk
wombs open to the flower
of my seed
this courtroom is filled
with witches
lovely as Delilah
slender as Salome
when the judge tastes
this much magic
when tongues speak names
of warty widows
bodies I would never touch
a rope braided in heaven
coils hard and tight in my fist

Outside

I stand outside the prison
a dungeon locked with lies
my wife is somewhere
behind the darkness
of the door
Susanah, my faithful bride
gone, gone, gone
a tortured ghost
held in chains
all day, all night
her soul breathes
in a grave I cannot find

now I know
where hell is

In the Dust

my words become weapons
accusals that drag death
through every room of this house
over floors I scrub, and wax and shine
the kitchen where I peel, and chop
and cook
parlour walls covered with red
tapestry of Elizabeth's art
John's quiet study
open Bible on his desk
he swings from a scaffold
no one to cut him down
Elizabeth cradles his son
in the hunger of her cell
their home is a tomb
my name, Mary Warren,
smeared in the dust

MISCARRIAGE

in a cell
too cold for breath
a woman miscarries
holds a stillborn
in her arms
blood bathes mother and child
soaks through a straw pallet
hemorrhages between iron bars
down the hall
past the midnight guard
a brilliant key
warm, wet and red
this eternal lullaby
opens rusted locks

COURT-COLD CRADLE

my infant, my baby, my newborn, my Mary
cries
in the court-cold cradle
of our Salem cell
I wrap my child
in prison rags
offer my small, stone-dry breast
weep an ancient song
soft, soft, soft

dawn brings only silence
the moon a hollow shell
my baby, my Mary, my pale blue shadow
dead as bone
sleep little one, sleep in my arms

FOUR-YEAR-OLD WITCH

I am chained
to walls of my mother's cell
left alone
when she is led
to a high hill
a narrow noose
fitted to her neck

I see my mother's eyes
feel their embrace
in the dark
clear blue light fades
into a shameful grave
without her
I am blind

PRISON DEATH

I have one torn blanket
in this small Salem cell
left by a witch
hanged in September storms
lightning and hail
hurled from a sky
black as Satan's soul

day and night
her spirit covers me
presence of a demon
or a saint
she whispers
that Gallow's Hill
will come to me
scents of hawthorn
will fill my lungs
close my throat
a young witch
wrapped in a thin blanket
woven into spring
her heart freed
of words still wet
on lips gone white

while the jailor sleeps
with every numbered key
gleaming on his chain

HUNGER AND THIRST

she stands at my door
Sarah Good
smell of rags
soiled with sweat
she asks for bread and tea
inhales biscuits rising
light and fresh and sweet

I turn her away
she steps backwards
sharp mutter of words
from a witch's tongue
she's accused
chained in a Salem cell
her belly bloated
ripe as birth
the jailer brings
milk and cheese
says the child
will not swing
from a wormy tree
the living cord
around her neck
tightens with hunger
twists with thirst

SKELETON

my husband brings
biscuits, apples, cheese, and tea
a folded shawl
knitted shades of love
he holds my hands
weeps for
a skeleton who can barely
swallow tea
Thomas feels the slip
of my wedding ring
our shining golden circle
broken
like bones of a slender neck
in the crush of a court
where laws strike mercy
from script and speech

the scaffold outside the door

FROM THE SCAFFOLD

the scorn of Salem
my hands snatch
hard crusts of charity
girls in spotless skirts
cut patterns for a witch
I am pinned in the centre
trapped in their web
my body the perfect fit
for a coarse prison dress

moments before death
my voice rises
into the sharp
curve of light
you are liars
my blood
spills from your mouths
dooms all your children
fields filled with coffins
flowers reaching up from
roots of hopeless graves

Early Frost

hawthorn needles sparkle
sing in the sun
clusters of light, like jewels
in a witch's hair
I, Bridget Byshop, tremble
on the scaffold
my cloak edged
with perfect French knots
removed
the hangman picks
a branch, sturdy enough
to hold a woman
take every living breath
until all that frozen
splendor fades into mist
a cold, damp veil
that falls
over my hair, my face

Choking on a Curse

silent as wolves
men circle my farm
a woman who harvests
gallons of honey
bushels of apples
crates of berries

they hang me high
choking on a curse
biting on a prayer
spirits of the tree
ease my slow
slow strangle
enough to steal
small sips of air

to stay awake

at first light
they cut me down
Mary Webster
a thirsty witch
who stares at
the man who
carried the rope
the neighbour who
tied my wrists

the one who sneered
at my skirts
watched the wind
uncover
long slender legs
all the magic between
yielding to his eye

WHEN MY MOTHER DIES

I kneel in my mother's room
one candle lights her table
a brush, a few small combs
ties for her lovely hair

in this hour my mother dies
the torment of her innocence
fills my mouth, throat and lungs
as if my body still breathes in hers
she begged me
not to come to Gallow's Hill
but from a distance
I hear the shouts
feel the panic, her pounding heart
struggling to stay
with me, to save me from
the eyes of her corpse
when I hold a lantern
search for my mother
around courthouse and jail
disgraced Puritan church

all the graveyards of this town

LAST BREATH OF LEAVES

the night
before my death
lightning slices though
branches of trees
on Gallow's Hill
from my cell
I hear the angry roar
of their fall
last breath of leaves

on the scaffold
rain pelts against my face
my frightened eyes
perfumed petals
from a killing tree
gather in my hair
a garland or a halo
the hangman's hands falter
a crown on the head
of a witch is an omen
he begs my forgiveness
while I still can speak

CHAINS

after a year
the jailor unlocks
chains stained with blood
women from the town
bathe me in hot water
scrub me raw
comb lice from
matted hair
scissored short

only five years old
and I can barely stand
I screech
like an animal
caught in the teeth
of a trap

I'll always be
alone in a cell
the keys lost
buried with my mother
in a hidden grave
covered with thistles
brambles and weeds

Doubt

there are those in the church
who begin to question
all these hangings
weight of death
heavy on the town
how could Rebecca Nurse, Mary Easty
and Martha Corey be witches
women who breathed
in the realm of God
fruits of their fields shared
with strangers in times
of famine and plague

maybe Salem's witches
are angels from Satan's choir
chanting in the courtroom
strumming lovely instruments
strings rubbed with resins
played with deceit

A WITCH WITH WINGS

a crazed mob points at me
Lady Mary, the governor's wife
a witch who'll never be naked
never chained in a foul cell
never alone on a scaffold
rotted with lies

this witch will fly
before a Boston judge
deny spectral witness
tear the court apart
rip out chapter and verse
laws signed with Satan's pen
burn them in Salem streets
where wild demons dance

ABIGAIL WILLIAMS IN BOSTON

was it a game I played
cards with nineteen names
nineteen faces
broken skulls staring
down at me
from ceilings of despair

I've run from Salem's Satan
to a papered room
in a Boston brothel
where men pay me
to undress
to offer myself
naked
they never ask
who I am
who I was
they only want
a witch tied to a post
who knows all the magic
of ropes and chains

Too Late

years after
my spasms and spells
vile voodoo charms
I stand in the same courtroom
to recant
names of women written
into a tragedy
of prison, false witness
betrayal of friend and kin
they come before me
skeletons suspended from trees
eyes missing
lips bitten to bone
hair woven into wild nests
of ravens and crows
I cannot reach up
to cover wasted bones
with all the colour of life
to offer the blessing
of my eyes
thick braids of hair
too late
for my testament
too late
for a young witch
to confess

ABSOLUTION

fifty years ago
my mother died
on Gallow's Hill
women held up
their children
to watch a witch
jump into hell
all of her power
lost in the flame
of God's holy word

today I hold a letter
from the governor
he names my mother
says her death
was an error
a misjudgment of the times
she was never a witch
never a threat

he sends money
to buy back
her house, her land

the house burned
in a lightning fire
her land flooded
in a storm
fifty years ago
my mother was sold
even her frail bones
are gone
broken into bits
chewed by vicious wolves

no one knows
the price

Playing Field

nineteen ghosts
spectators on Gallow's Hill
haunted eyes looking down
on every football game
keeping score

hawthorn branches
suspend us
high above the playing field
ripe-red berries
long, toothy thorns
blooms shaped like skirts
stretched into shrouds
specter of nineteen witches
who drew eager crowds
for a favoured Salem sport
stakes high as any tree
cheap as a witch's breath

GLOSSARY

Byshop, Bridget: Hanged July 10, 1692. Bridget was a widow and owner of two successful taverns outside of Salem. She could afford to dress in fashionable Parisian styles, for which she was greatly criticized in the ultra-conservative Puritan culture. Bridget's brother-in-law coveted her wealth, and, along with the afflicted girls, accused her of witchcraft.

Corey, Martha: Hanged September 22, 1692. Martha was a wife, mother, and was active in the Puritan congregation, who often read from the Bible in services. She spoke publicly against the belief in witches. She was ultimately accused by Abigail Williams and Ann Putnam.

Easty, Mary: Hanged September 22, 1692. Mary was a widow and respected member of the Puritan Church. She wrote a statement of innocence upon her accusation, which was disregarded by the judges; the testimony of the afflicted girls was stronger than hers.

Good, Sarah: Hanged July 19, 1692. Sarah was considered to be a beggar and a social misfit, and was an easy target for accusation of witchcraft. After her trial, she gave birth to a child, Mary, who died in the prison. Her four-year-old-daughter, Dorcas, was chained in the dungeon prison for almost a year, and became mentally unstable.

Hobbs, Deliverance: Deliverance was accused by her own daughter, Abigail. She confessed and was not hanged. Confession was viewed as a way to escape the gallows, but always implicated other women and kept the belief in witches alive.

Nurse, Rebecca: Hanged July 19, 1692. Rebecca was a seventy-year-old widow and an upstanding member of the Puritan community. Rebecca was deaf and could not hear the questions being asked of her in court; her silences were interpreted as guilt.

Osborne, Sarah: Died in prison, 1692. Sarah tried to break the conditions of her dead husband's will, thereby depriving his sons of a large farm. She turned the farm over to her new husband, Thomas Osborne. This was scandalous in Salem, and is most likely the reason she was accused. Sarah died in prison shackles at the age of forty-nine as a result of extreme prison conditions.

Parris, Betty: Betty was the daughter of the minister Samuel Parris. She was only six years old when she started exhibiting very strange behaviours, which a physician attributed to the influence of a witch. As a result, her father spread the fear of witches from his pulpit. Betty moved away and her health improved. Later, she married and had four children.

Phips, Lady Mary: Lady Mary was the wife of Governor William Phips. When she was accused, Governor Phips abolished "spectral witness" as evidence of witchcraft. On Oct. 29, 1692, he stopped arrests and hangings, dissolved the courts, and released several prisoners. This ended the witch-craze in Salem.

Proctor, John and Elizabeth: John was a tavern owner who openly denounced the witchcraft trials, thus making him a target. He and his wife, Elizabeth, were both accused by Mary Warren. John Proctor was hanged. Elizabeth's pregnancy saved her from the gallows.

Pudeater, Ann: Hanged September 22, 1692. As a midwife and property owner, she was highly vulnerable to accusations of witchcraft. Ann was also a seventy-year-old widow, making her a match for the profile of a witch.

Putnam, Ann: Ann was a member of the prosperous Putnam family of Salem. At twelve years of age, she was the youngest accuser and is the only girl who recanted and made a public apology for the great injustice she had perpetrated on innocent women.

Tituba: Tituba was an Indian woman from Barbados, and a slave owned by Samuel Parris. She was one of the most powerful influences on the afflicted girls, who believed she could tell their futures and that she had knowledge of voodoo. When accused of witchcraft, Tituba confessed but also named Sarah Good and Sarah Osborne as witches. Because Tituba confessed early on, and because she named other women, she avoided trial and was not hanged.

Warren, Mary: Mary was a servant in the home of John and Elizabeth Proctor. Mary, like Abigail Williams, was an orphan as a result of the American Indian Wars; she was also greatly influenced by Tituba. Mary accused John and Elizabeth Proctor as well as several others.

Webster, Mary: Hanged 1695, cut down while still alive. Mary was accused of witchcraft and left to hang all night. In the morning, she was cut down, still alive, and lived fourteen more years. It is not known how she survived the hanging. Superstitious neighbours became afraid that nothing could kill her, and left her alone. She was an ancestor to the Canadian writer, Margaret Atwood, who wrote a poem, "Half-Hanged Mary."

Williams, Abigail: Abigail was an orphan and a servant in the home of Samuel Parris. She was influenced by Tituba and was one of the main accusers of witches. When doubt of the validity of the girls' accusations became stronger in Salem, Abigail left. It is thought that she later became a prostitute in Boston.

The Afflicted Girls: Elizabeth Booth, Elizabeth Hubbard, Mercy Lewis, Elizabeth Parris, Ann Putnam, Mary Walcott, Mary Warren, Abigail Williams.